LAUGH OUT LOUD!

THE FUNNY FOOD JOKE BOOK

Sean Connolly and Kay Barnham

WINDMILL
BOOKS

New York

Published in 2012 by Windmill Books, LLC
303 Park Avenue South, Suite # 1280, New York, NY 10010-3657

First Edition

Editor: Joe Harris
Illustrations: Adam Clay and Dynamo Design
Layout Design: Notion Design

Library of Congress Cataloging-in-Publication Data

Connolly, Sean, 1956–
  The funny food joke book / by Sean Connolly and Kay Barnham. — 1st ed.
      p. cm. — (Laugh out loud!)
  Includes index.
  ISBN 978-1-61533-365-3 (library binding) — ISBN 978-1-61533-403-2 (pbk.) — ISBN 978-1-61533-466-7
(6-pack)
  1. Food—Juvenile humor. I. Barnham, Kay. II. Title.
  PN6231.F66C66 2012
  818'.602—dc22
                                    2010052138

Printed in China

For more great fiction and nonfiction, go to www.windmillbooks.com

CPSIA Compliance Information: Batch #AS2011WM: For Further Information contact Windmill Books, New York, New York at 1-866-478-0556
SL001839US

CONTENTS

FUNNY FOOD

Why did the cookie cry?
Because his mom had
been a wafer
so long.

When do truck drivers stop for a snack?
When they see a fork in the road.

What did one plate say to the other plate?
Lunch is on me.

Knock knock.
Who's there?
Cash.
Cash who?
No, thanks. I prefer walnuts.

Why did the rhubarb go out with a prune?
Because he couldn't find a date.

FUNNY FOOD

This coffee is disgusting—it tastes like mud.
I'm not surprised—it was ground a few minutes ago!

Why did the chef serve frozen steak?
He wanted it to melt in the mouth.

What do you get if you cross a comedian and an orange?
Peels of laughter.

What do you call an airplane passenger covered in salt and pepper?
A seasoned traveler.

What did the speedy tomato say to the slow tomato?
Ketchup!

FUNNY FOOD

What happened at the cannibals' wedding?
They toasted the bride and groom.

Waiter, waiter, there's a button in my lettuce.
Ah! That will be from the salad dressing, sir!

Why did the man eat yeast and furniture polish for breakfast?
He wanted to rise and shine.

Knock knock.
Who's there?
Arthur.
Arthur who?
Arthur any cookies left?

How do you make
a fruit punch?
Give it boxing lessons.

FUNNY FOOD

Why did the girl stare at the orange juice carton?
Because it said "concentrate" on the label.

Why was the chef so relaxed?
He had plenty of thyme on his hands!

What's yellow and dangerous?
Shark-infested custard.

Waiter, waiter—there's a fly in my soup!
Sorry, madam, I didn't know you were vegetarian!

Did you hear about the Thanksgiving turkey who tried to escape the roasting pan?
He was foiled.

FUNNY FOOD

What do you get if you cross a Shakespeare play and an egg?
Omelet!

How do you know when a cannibal feels like eating you?
He keeps buttering you up!

What did the fat man say when he sat down at the dinner table?
"Just think—all this food is going to waist!"

How do you make gold soup?
Put 14 carrots in it!

What do you get if you divide the circumference of a pumpkin by its diameter?
Pumpkin pi.

FUNNY FOOD

A pizza walks into a bar and asks for a burger.
"I'm sorry," says the barman.
"We don't serve food."

Chef: I didn't use a recipe for this casserole—I made it up out of my own head!
Customer: I thought it tasted of sawdust!

If I cut a potato in two, I have two halves. If I cut a potato in four, I have four quarters. What do I have if I cut a potato in sixteen?
French fries!

Why did the bakers work late?
Because they kneaded the dough!

How much did the pirate pay for his corn?
A buck an ear.

FUNNY FOOD

Waiter, can I have my lunch on the patio?
Certainly, sir, but most people find a plate more sensible!

Why should you never tell secrets in a corn field?
Because you would be surrounded by ears!

What farm animal can you spread on toast?
A baby goat – it's a little butter!

What's the most expensive item on the menu at a Chinese restaurant?
Fortune cookies.

Mmmmm! This cake is lovely and warm!
It should be; the cat's been sitting on it all afternoon!

FUNNY FOOD

What do computer
operators eat for a snack?
Chips!

How do they eat their chips?
One byte at a time.

Which snack is wicked and
lives in the desert?
The sand witch!

How do you keep flies out of
your kitchen?
Move the pile of rotting vegetables into the living room!

What starts and ends with "t," and is also full of "t?"
A teapot.

What kind of bird is at every meal?
A swallow.

FUNNY FOOD

Why did the vampire always
carry a bottle of tomato
ketchup?
He was a vegetarian!

What is the one thing that stays
hot in the refrigerator?
Mustard!

What did the chewing gum say
to the shoe?
I'm stuck on you.

Why did the beet blush?
Because he saw the salad
dressing.

Knock knock.
Who's there?
Phil.
Phil who?
Phil this cup with sugar, would you, I've run out!

FUNNY FOOD

What do you get if you boil up 25 cars, three buses, and a truckload of sugar?
Traffic jam.

Why is cutting a slice of gingerbread the easiest job in the world?
It's a piece of cake.

What is the best time to pick apples?
When the farmer is away on vacation!

Customer: Why is there a dead fly in my soup?
Waiter: Well, you surely don't expect to get a live one at these prices!

What did one snowman say to the other snowman?
Smells like carrots.

FUNNY FOOD

Why did the man send his alphabet soup back?
Because he couldn't find words to describe it!

Did you hear about the silly farmer who took his cows to the North Pole, thinking he would get ice cream?

Waiter—there's half a dead cockroach in my food!
You'll have to pay for the half you've eaten, sir!

How do you eat your Thanksgiving turkey?
I just gobble it down!

Did you hear about the eggs who kept playing tricks on people?
They were practical yolkers.

FUNNY FOOD

Why do bees have icky, sticky hair?
They use honeycombs.

Waiter—this crab only has one claw!
Sorry, sir, it must have been in a fight!
In that case, take it away and bring me the winner.

Doctor, I think I've just swallowed a chicken bone!
Are you choking?
No, I'm serious!

What do you call a lazy baker?
A loafer!

Waiter, this omelet tastes awful!
Sir, I can assure you that our chef has been making omelets since he was a child!
That may be true, but can I have one of his fresher ones please?

FUNNY FOOD

Why did the lemon refuse to fight the orange?
Because it was yellow!

There's a stick insect in my salad—fetch me the branch manager at once!

Where is the best place to keep a pie?
Your tummy!

What type of lettuce did they serve on the Titanic?
Iceberg.

FUNNY FOOD

Did you hear about the paranoid potatoes?
They kept their eyes peeled for danger.

Why do basketball players love doughnuts?
They can dunk them.

Why are seagulls called seagulls?
Because if they flew over bays, they would be bagels.

What did the carrot stick say to the potato chip?
"Want to go for a dip?"

What sort of dog has no tail?
A hot dog!

FUNNY FOOD

What do trash collectors eat?
Junk food.

Teacher: Sally, give me a sentence with the word "aroma" in it!
Sally: My uncle Fred is always traveling; he's aroma!

Teacher: Philip, why do you have a lunchbox in each hand?
Pupil: It's important to have a balanced diet, Mr. Harrison!

What do you get if you mix birdseed with your breakfast cereal?
Shredded tweet.

What is worse than finding a worm in your apple?
Finding half a worm in your apple!

FUNNY FOOD

What's a cannibal's
favorite takeout?
Pizza with
everyone on it.

What did the
golfer eat for
lunch?
A sand wedge.

Why are clocks greedy?
They always have seconds.

Why couldn't Batman go fishing?
Because Robin had eaten all the worms.

Did you hear about the strawberry who attended charm
school?
He became a real smoothie.

Which part of Swiss cheese is the least fattening?
The holes!

FUNNY FOOD

What do you call a pig that does karate?
A pork chop.

Why did the potato cry?
Its peelings were hurt.

How do you make a stiff drink?
Put cement in your cup.

Did you hear about Professor Cole, the scientist who discovered the perfect ratio for mixing cabbage, carrot, onion, and mayonnaise?
He called it Cole's Law.

Why did the girl disappear into the bowl of granola?
A strong currant pulled her under.

FUNNY FOOD

Knock knock.
Who's there?
Police.
Police who?
Police can I have a chocolate milkshake?

What kind of nut always has a cold?
A cashew!

What do you call a fake noodle?
An impasta.

Johnny! How many more times do I have
to tell you to keep away from the
cookie jar?
No more times—it's
empty!

What do you get if you
cross a chicken with a
cement mixer?
A bricklayer.

FUNNY FOOD

Does Dracula's chef ever cook roast beef?
Yes, but very rarely.

What is a chicken's favorite dessert?
Layer cake!

Knock knock.
Who's there?
Anita.
Anita who?
Anita nother hot dog—I'm starving!

How do you fix a broken
pizza?
With tomato paste!

Why did the man
wear a
banana skin
on each foot?
He wanted a
pair of
slippers.

FUNNY FOOD

Our school lunches are untouched by human hand—there's a gorilla in the kitchen!

Why is a birthday cake like a golf ball? They both get sliced.

Why are baked beans and onions dangerous? Together they make tear gas.

Knock knock.
Who's there?
Army.
Army who?
Army and you still going for ice cream?

Waiter, do you serve crabs?
Relax, sir. We serve anybody.

23

FUNNY FOOD

Where do hamburgers dance?
At meatballs.

What is the frying pan's favorite song?
"Home on the Range."

Why did the turkey cross the road?
It was the chicken's day off.

I'm on a seafood diet. The more I see food, the
more I eat!

FUNNY FOOD

What did the grape say when someone trod on it?
It let out a little whine.

What did one strawberry say to the other?
"Look at the jam you've gotten us into!"

What do you call a woman with a nut tree on her head?
Hazel.

Why did Mrs. Grape leave Mr. Grape?
Because she was tired of raisin kids.

Waiter! There's a fly in my soup!
Yes, sir, it's the bad meat that attracts them.

What are apricots?
Where baby monkeys sleep.

FUNNY FOOD

We don't let Dad near the kitchen. The last time he cooked, he burned the salad!

Waiter, will my pizza be long?
No, it will be round.

What do you call a cow with three legs?
Lean beef.

What's the difference between a butcher and an insomniac?
One weighs a steak and the other stays awake.

What do you get from nervous cows?
Milkshakes!

FUNNY FOOD

What did one knife say to the other knife?
"Look sharp!"

Knock knock.
Who's there?
Wilma.
Wilma who?
Wilma lunch
be ready
soon?

Why aren't pancakes
any good at basketball?
Too many turnovers.

What did baby corn say to
Mommy corn?
Where's popcorn?

What do you call stolen candy?
Hot chocolate.

FUNNY FOOD

What do you get if
you cross a turkey
with an octopus?
Eight drumsticks
for Thanksgiving
dinner.

Why did the man fill
his waterbed with
root beer?
Because he wanted
a foam mattress.

Waiter, this food isn't fit for a pig.
I'm sorry sir; I'll bring you some that is.

What is a cannibal's favourite game?
Swallow the leader.

What do chimps wear when they're cooking?
Ape-rons!

FUNNY FOOD

What is lemonade?
When you help an elderly lemon cross the road.

Waiter—this food is terrible. Bring me the manager.
I'm sorry, sir. He won't eat it either.

You can eat dirt cheap at the local diner!
Maybe so, but who wants to eat dirt?

Waiter, there's a hand in my soup.
That's not your soup, sir, it's the finger bowl.

If it looks like a duck, walks like a duck, and talks like a duck... it probably needs a little more time in the oven.

FUNNY FOOD

What do you get if you cross a shark with a hen?
Chicken of the Sea.

What did the octopus hate about eating every night?
Washing his hands before dinner.

Which is the most musical fish?
The piano tuna.

Customer: Waiter, could you please tell me what I've just eaten?
Waiter: Why do you ask, sir?
Customer: Because I'll need to tell the doctor soon!

Where do the toughest, meanest chickens come from?
From hard-boiled eggs.

FUNNY FOOD

If vegetarians eat vegetables, does that mean that humanitarians eat humans?

Waiter, waiter, have you smoked salmon?
No, sir, but I have smoked a pipe.

What does a billionaire make for dinner every night?
Reservations.

Waiter—is there soup on the menu?
No, sir. I wiped it off.

What do you call a man in a huge pot?
Stu.

Glossary

byte (BITE) a measurement of information on a computer

circumference (sur-KUM-frens) the distance around a circle

diameter (dy-A-muh-tur) the width of a circle

humanitarian (hyoo-MAN-ih-TEHR-ee-un) someone who tries to keep people from suffering

insomniac (in-SOM-nee-ak) someone who cannot sleep

paranoid (PAR-uh-noyd) worried that everyone wants to harm you

Further Reading

Bozzo, Linda. *Food Jokes to Tickle Your Funny Bone*. Berkeley Height, NJ: Enslow Publishers, 2011.

Dahl, Michael. *Chuckle Squad*. Mankato, MN: Picture Window Books, 2010.

Winter, Judy A. *Jokes About Food*. Mankato, MN: Capstone Press, 2010.

Index

Web Sites

For Web resources related to the subject of this book, go to: www.windmillbooks.com/weblinks and select this book's title.